# A GRAPHIC HISTORY OF THE AMERICAN WEST

# THE EXPLORATIONS
## OF LEWIS AND CLARK

BY GARY JEFFREY
ILLUSTRATED BY TERRY RILEY

**Gareth Stevens**
Publishing

Please visit our website, www.garethstevens.com.
For a free color catalog of all our high-quality books,
call toll free 1-800-542-2595 or fax 1-877-542-2596.

Library of Congress Cataloging-in-Publication Data

Jeffrey, Gary.
The explorations of Lewis and Clark / Gary Jeffrey.
p. cm. — (A graphic history of the American West)
Includes index.
ISBN 978-1-4339-6737-5 (pbk.)
ISBN 978-1-4339-6738-2 (6-pack)
ISBN 978-1-4339-6735-1 (library binding)
1. Lewis and Clark Expedition (1804-1806)—Juvenile literature. 2. West
(U.S.)—Discovery and exploration—Juvenile literature. 3. Lewis,
Meriwether, 1774-1809—Juvenile literature. 4. Clark, William, 1770-
1838—Juvenile literature. I. Title.
F592.7.J44 2012
917.804'2—dc23
2011022748

First Edition

Published in 2012 by
**Gareth Stevens Publishing**
111 East 14th Street, Suite 349
New York, NY 10003

*Designed by* David West Books

Photo credits:
P5b, 3395 cliff1066™; p22b, b r e n t

Printed in China

CPSIA compliance information: Batch #DW12GS: For further information contact Gareth Stevens, New York, New York at 1-800-542-2595.

# CONTENTS

# A New Frontier

President Thomas Jefferson had long wanted to explore the wilderness of the Louisiana Territory that lay west of the states. In 1803, he began organizing an expedition up the Missouri River to be led by his private secretary, Captain Meriwether Lewis.

*Beyond Missouri's settlements lay an uncharted world.*

*Jefferson admired Lewis's bravery and good judgement– important qualities in an explorer.*

*Jefferson hoped his expedition would find a river route to the Pacific that could be used to trade with the Orient.*

## A Special Purchase

The Louisiana Territory had been claimed by the French, but barring a few trappers, almost no Europeans lived there. When Jefferson tried to buy the port of New Orleans, the French surprised him by offering the entire territory for sale! Jefferson accepted. At a pen stroke, the size of the U.S.A. was doubled overnight.

*As well as leader, Clark would also serve as an expedition medic.*

*It was known that Native Americans hunted buffalo on the Great Plains of the West, but not much else.*

## TWO LEADERS

Lewis was a capable soldier and first-class natural historian, but the expedition had become too big and important for one man to lead alone. He was joined by ex-soldier William Clark. They would lead the expedition as joint captains. Clark would take care of the mapmaking while Lewis would collect information on plants and animals. Both men had excellent leadership and wilderness skills. The thirty-three expedition members would become known as the Corps of Discovery.

## NATIVE LANDS

Their aim was to travel the Missouri River to its source and find a route across the Rockies to the Pacific. They set off in May 1804 from St. Louis in a large keelboat and two pirogues. Heading deep into Native American country, they hoped the welcome would be friendly…

*Peace medals bearing Jefferson's head would be offered to Native American chiefs.*

# THE EXPLORATIONS OF LEWIS AND CLARK

SEPTEMBER 25, 1804. ON THE EASTERN EDGE OF THE GREAT PLAINS, TETON SIOUX WARRIORS BARRED THE WAY.

HE'S ASKING FOR THE BOAT. HE'S NOT SATISFIED WITH THE GIFTS.

NO WAY!

THE YOUNG SIOUX CHIEF BECAME THREATENING. CLARK DREW HIS SWORD. LEWIS AIMED THE SHIP'S GUN...

ALL MEN BE UNDER ARMS!

LUCKILY, THE GRAND CHIEF STEPPED IN AND DEFUSED THE SITUATION.

SOON THEY WERE ON THEIR WAY...

THERE'S DEFINITELY BAD BLOOD BETWEEN US AND THE TETON.

YES, AND WE WILL HAVE TO PASS THROUGH THEM IF WE TAKE THIS ROUTE HOME.

THEIR JOURNEY UP THE MISSOURI WAS A RACE AGAINST THE COMING WINTER.

WE'VE GOT TO REACH THE MANDAN VILLAGE BEFORE THE RIVER FREEZES.

UNLIKE THEIR SIOUX COUSINS, THE MANDANS LIVED IN A PERMANENT SETTLEMENT ON THE RIVERBANK.

AT THE MANDAN VILLAGE, THE CORPS BUILT A FORT...

...IN CASE THE TETONS COME LOOKING!

WHEN FOOD RAN LOW, THEY HUNTED BUFFALO ON THE PLAINS.

BANG!

MEANWHILE, LEWIS AND CLARK COLLECTED SUPPLIES AND MADE DUGOUT CANOES TO REPLACE THE KEELBOAT. THEY WERE ABOUT TO GO WHERE NO WHITE AMERICAN HAD EVER BEEN.

UPRIVER ON MAY 5. LEWIS, WHO HAD SHOT AND WOUNDED A GRIZZLY, GOT A FRIGHT WHEN ITS COMPANION TURNED ON HIM.

GRAAAAGH!

RELOAD - AND QUICKLY!

THE BEAR WAS DOWNED JUST IN TIME.

CRACK!

JUNE 3. THEY CAME TO AN UNCHARTED FORK IN THE RIVER.

SIRS, WE ALL BELIEVE THE NORTH FORK IS THE MISSOURI.

WELL, WE CHOOSE THE SOUTH.

THE SOUTH FORK IS CLEARER, LIKE IT COMES FROM THE MOUNTAINS.

THEY WERE SEARCHING FOR THE FABLED FALLS OF THE MISSOURI.

BY JUNE 16, THEY HAD FOUND THE FALLS, WHICH TURNED OUT TO BE JUST ONE OF A SERIES OF **FIVE**.

I KNEW WE WOULD HAVE TO **PORTAGE**, BUT THIS IS RIDICULOUS.

**PORTAGE** MEANT CARRYING THE BOATS **AROUND** THE FALLS. TRUCKS WERE MADE TO **WHEEL** THEM ACROSS THE PRAIRIES.

THEY WERE CLIMBING THE ROCKIES BY A RIVER ROUTE, BUT TO GET ACROSS THE CONTINENTAL DIVIDE, THEY WOULD NEED **HORSES**...

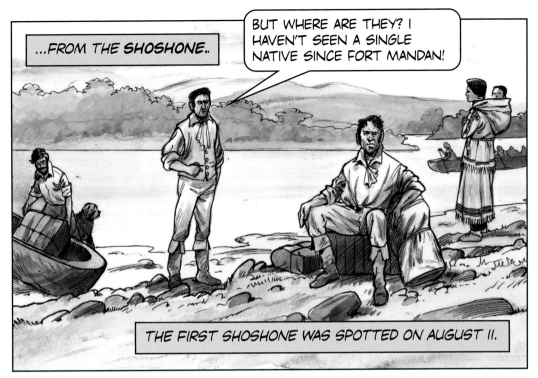

...FROM THE **SHOSHONE**..

BUT WHERE ARE THEY? I HAVEN'T SEEN A SINGLE NATIVE SINCE FORT MANDAN!

THE FIRST SHOSHONE WAS SPOTTED ON AUGUST 11.

ON AUGUST 17, THEY HAD A MEETING WITH THE SHOSHONE CHIEF, AT WHICH SACAGAWEA REVEALED A **SURPRISE**.

CAPTAIN CLARK, THE CHIEF IS MY **BROTHER**.

THE CORPS TRADED FOR HORSES AND SUPPLIES. THE SHOSHONE DROVE A HARD BARGAIN.

AN OLD SHOSHONE ALSO OFFERED TO GUIDE THEM ON A TRAIL THAT WAS USED BY THE NEZ PERCE, WHO LIVED ON THE FAR SIDE OF THE ROCKIES.

"WE HAVE NOW LEFT THE LOUISIANA PURCHASE AND HAVE ENTERED THE DISPUTED* OREGON COUNTRY."

ACROSS THE BITTERROOT MOUNTAINS, THE GOING GOT TOUGH.

"ELEVEN HARD DAYS. SEVERAL HORSES STARVED TO DEATH, HUMANS FARING LITTLE BETTER."

* DISPUTED WITH BRITAIN.

14

FINALLY, THEY MET UP WITH THE NEZ PERCE, WHO FED THE STARVING EXPLORERS AND HELPED BUILD DUGOUTS FOR THE JOURNEY DOWN THE CLEARWATER RIVER.

WE'LL HAVE THE CURRENT BEHIND US. NOTHING CAN STOP US NOW.

WOOF!

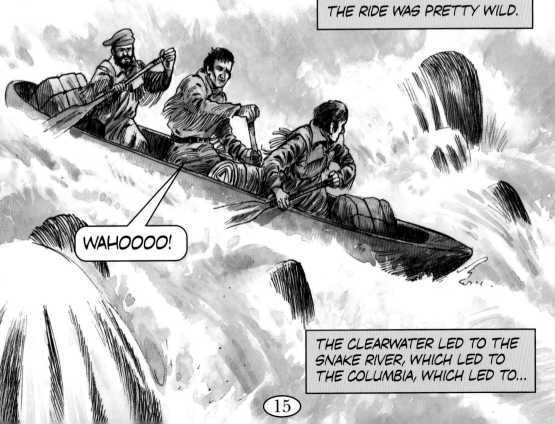

THE RIDE WAS PRETTY WILD.

WAHOOOO!

THE CLEARWATER LED TO THE SNAKE RIVER, WHICH LED TO THE COLUMBIA, WHICH LED TO...

...THE PACIFIC!

LOOK AT THE ROLLERS – IT'S MARVELOUS!

IT WAS NOVEMBER 20. FROM THE MOUTH OF THE MISSOURI, THEY HAD TRAVELED 3,700 MILES (5,955 KILOMETERS). THEIR MISSION WAS OVER. WITH NO SIGHT OF A SHIP TO CARRY THEM HOME, THE CAPTAINS DECIDED TO MAKE A CAMP.

THE DAYS PASSED BY SLOWLY AT FORT CLATSOP.

AFTER WEEKS OF RAIN AND NO SHIP, THEY DECIDED TO GO BACK BY LAND.

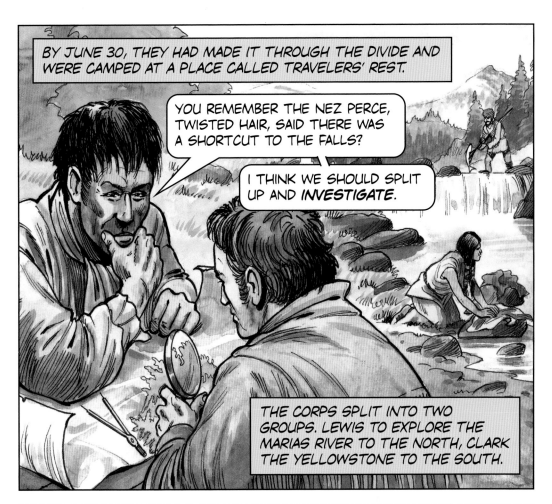

BY JUNE 30, THEY HAD MADE IT THROUGH THE DIVIDE AND WERE CAMPED AT A PLACE CALLED TRAVELERS' REST.

YOU REMEMBER THE NEZ PERCE, TWISTED HAIR, SAID THERE WAS A SHORTCUT TO THE FALLS?

I THINK WE SHOULD SPLIT UP AND *INVESTIGATE*.

THE CORPS SPLIT INTO TWO GROUPS. LEWIS TO EXPLORE THE MARIAS RIVER TO THE NORTH, CLARK THE YELLOWSTONE TO THE SOUTH.

JULY 27. LEWIS'S GROUP GOT INTO A FIGHT WITH SOME BLACKFEET INDIANS WHO WERE CAUGHT STEALING GUNS AND HORSES.

TWO BLACKFEET WARRIORS WERE KILLED.

THE END

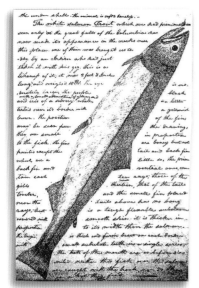

*Journal entries included highly detailed drawings of wildlife and plants.*

Lewis and Clark kept a detailed journal throughout their trip. With this and through their eyewitness accounts, they were able to satisfy Jefferson's curiosity about the Far West. They became heroes and household names in their lifetimes.

## AMERICAN DISCOVERIES

Sadly, their journey had put paid to the notion of a northwest river passage. The mountains were just too high. What they did bring back was information. They had close contact with more than 16 different tribes and had discovered about 200 animals and plants that were unknown to white America, including the gray wolf and grizzly bear.

*This memorial includes the figure of Lewis's Newfoundland dog, Seaman.*

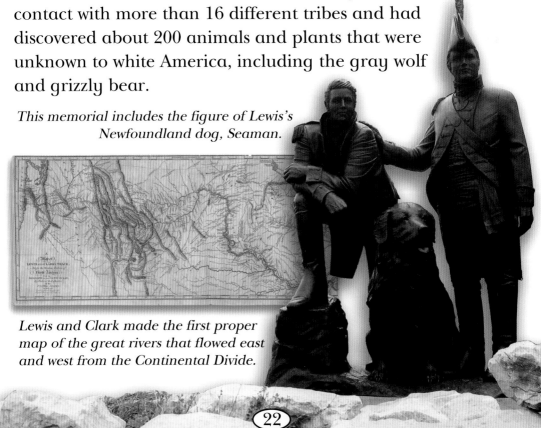

*Lewis and Clark made the first proper map of the great rivers that flowed east and west from the Continental Divide.*

# GLOSSARY

**Continental Divide** The point in the Rocky Mountains where water stops flowing into either the Atlantic or Pacific Ocean and starts flowing into the other.

**defuse** To make a situation less dangerous or hostile.

**dugouts** Dugout canoes made from hollowed-out tree trunks.

**keelboat** A large, flat freight boat used on rivers.

**notion** An idea or belief.

**pirogue** A small, flat-bottomed boat used in Louisiana that could be paddled into inaccessible areas.

**put paid to** To put an end to something, to settle it.

**recruit** To engage people to work, often in military service.

**revenge** To inflict punishment in return for an injury or wrongdoing.

**run the gauntlet** To run a risk of being attacked by opponents along a route.

**trapper** A person who earned their living trapping animals and trading their fur in exchange for other goods.

**uncharted** Not marked or recorded on a map or plan.

# INDEX